I WAS SO LUCKY

THE LIFE OF MARTIN HOLLAY

AS TOLD TO TOM McGOWAN

I WAS SO LUCKY

THE LIFE OF MARTIN HOLLAY

ISBN: 0-9762108-5-6
ISBN13: 978-0-9762108-5-1

Design and Layout by Jannetje Anita Thomas, Photobooks Plus, LLC
www.photobooksplus.com

Images and photos by © Tom McGowan, Barbara Churchill, Martin Hollay and Photos.com

First printing: 2010

Printed in South Lake Tahoe, CA

United States

DEDICATED TO PRISCILLA HOLLAY

A Word at the Beginning

I have known Martin for only twelve of his ninety years. I have skied with him, camped with him, sailed with him, hiked with him and clinked a stampedli or two. Over those twelve years, I have become increasingly convinced that Martin Hollay is Tahoe Royalty.

His wonderful smile and spirit shine before him wherever he goes. When he enters a room, any room, most of those present call his name aloud.

The better I got to know him, the more I realized his extraordinary life story should be saved and shared. Over the past two years I have spent many, many hours sitting at his kitchen table with my tape recorder as he shared his amazingly detailed memories.

The book you hold in your hands will hopefully transport you to that kitchen table and allow you to experience Martin's story just as he told it. With the exception of re-arranging for continuity, I have transcribed his words exactly as he spoke them as to do otherwise would deny the reader the flavor of the man.

Throughout our conversations, Martin repeatedly told me how lucky he has been. In spite of some of the awful things he has experienced, he has always remained optimistic and grateful.

May some of that attitude and spirit lighten and enlighten your life as you enjoy "I Was So Lucky."

Tom McGowan
Lake Tahoe, Nevada
April, 2010

Martin!

The Start of it All

Martin

Well, I was born Martin Holl in Hungary on the first of November of 1920 in a little town next to Budapest, the capital, called Budakeszi. About 10 kilometers over the hill from Budapest.

That hill was where I skied first when I was about ten years old. My uncle made me a pair of wooden skis because it was easy to do it because not too far away was a business who made wine barrels and he picked up a small wine barrel and curved it up in the front, you know, and we took broken broom handles. We went up on the little hill and pushed us down just straight and that was our skiing. Who skis out further. No turning.

Tom - You begin by telling me when and where you were born and then immediately start talking about skiing.

Martin

Well, yes.

Tom - Did your mother and father ski?

No, just my uncle. Yes. Well then, later on he made a little business going up on the ski hill where every weekend the people came up skiing you know. We carried up two saw horses, two irons and a small bag of charcoal. I had the fire going and one of the irons and I had to yell: "Waxing! Waxing! The snow is sticking. Waxing! The snow is sticking. After ten cents you gonna slide better." That was my first ski job.

How long was the run on that hill?

On the little hill, just like you go up at Heavenly at World Cup, half way up and down that was our first little hill. We had 500 meters above sea level and we had plenty snow that time. That was way back in the 30's, you know. We walk up, no chairs, no rope tows and things like this. Ski down and walk back up.

MAKING TURNS, 1935

7

What do you remember of the little town of Budakeszi where you were born and your very early childhood?

Well, the little town was, I tell you, it was all Germans. It was a German settlement for way 200 years before when they called from Austria and Germany for settlers to come in because at that time Hungary was occupied by the Turks and they got rid of the Turks and then there was a country and no population. Yes.

There my family came from (Germany) and they settled down in Buda. At that time was Buda, and that's why they call them Budakeszi, and quite a few towns Buda this…, Buda that…, Buda… Whatever Buda means I don't know. It came from the way back when the Hungarians settled down a thousand years ago. I think Buda was one of the leaders of the settlement. Yes.

Did you live in the same house the whole time you were in Budakeszi?

Budakeszi. Yes. The house is still there where I was born. One of my cousins lives still in the house. Yes.

I never talked Hungarian when I was small, you know. The whole town was German. I learned Hungarian in the school when I was four or five years old. We spoke only German at home and my grand folks, they never talked Hungarian, just German. They understand Hungarian but they never spoke. They never went to school to learn Hungarian. When my mother went to school in, let's see, 1910, then they sent Hungarian teachers to the town and they was teaching Hungarian.

MARTIN'S GRANDFATHER

Were your mother and father born in Budakeszi and how about your grandparents?

Yes. And I think my grandparents were born there too in the 1870's. Yes. My father's folks they was born in 1870-1871 and my mother's folks they was 1872-1873. That's as far as I know it. My dad was born in 1896 and my mother born in 1899.

And then came the First World War. Father was 18 years old when he had to go to the war. He came home in 1920 and married my mother and that's when I was born. Our family name was Holl; a German name. At that time people thought it was better to have a more Hungarian sounding name so father changed our name to Hollai.

MARTIN'S FATHER

My father was a hero in the war. There was a hill in Italy and the Italian army had machine guns on it. My dad's unit couldn't go forward because the machine guns held them down. My dad and two other guys went all the way around to the other side of the hill and went up from the back. Then they got the machine guns. My dad told me then he took one of the Italians by the ear and lead him over to the Hungarian leader. That was funny.

When dad came home, he had the medals for being a hero but there weren't any records of them. Finally, after 15 years, dad found his old commander, Boncos Miklos. Miklos came to Budapest and told what my father had done so dad was finally officially a hero. I have his medal. It has the emblem of Hungary on it.

The President of Hungary, Vitez Horthi Miklos, did a ceremony by putting his sword on my father's shoulder to honor him into the order of the Vitez. (Hero) As the first son of my father, I knelt down with him and the president put his sword on my shoulder too. My dad was so proud.

Had your mother and father known each other as kids in the town?

Oh, yes. When they grew up they didn't live far from each other.

Now when you were a little boy living in Budakeszi did you ever go to Budapest?

Oh yes. I was in Budapest when I was six or eight years old with my mother and my brother and we walked over the hill to the end station of the streetcar from Budapest, you know, and we heard the street car noise and oh, then we saw the streetcar. Oh, it was a big thing to us, you know because we never saw a streetcar, of course. Then the people who arrived on the streetcar, we walked back home with them.

When we lived in Budakeszi, my brother was making a sword for school out of wood. He was playing with it and stabbed himself. We had a carriage with a horse to haul him in for ten kilometers to Budapest to the hospital but was inside blood. He was eight. I remember that was very sad.

MARTIN'S MOTHER

A BIKE RIDE - MARTIN ON LEFT

CROSS COUNTRY - MARTIN ON RIGHT

MARTIN GOES OUT ALONE IN THE KAYAK
AND BRINGS BACK TWO LOVELIES, 1939

Budapest and the Boy Scouts

BOY SCOUTS, 1933
MARTIN ON LEFT

In 1932 we moved into Budapest. My mom got a job as a maid in a big villa working for rich people, you know, as a housekeeper. Special laundry and ironing. It took a whole week just to do their ironing.

What did your father do for work?

My father was a bricklayer in Budapest, building houses out of bricks. In Budakeszi, they build their own houses already. For working they were cutting woods for firewood in the home.

You're still doing that.

Yes.

My father was famous when they build the villas on the hillsides all the rocks they made a stone wall. And one guy he delivered the rocks and they were raw. So my father had to work with the chisel and make the nice rounds and set them straight in a line. Put them together nicely.

When I go home now, I usually see them because I had to deliver lunch to him and I know where he was working and I look on the walls and have good memories about my dad. They worked by square foot so sometimes he made more money if was easy wall or sometimes less.

Did your sister go to school in Budapest?

Yes. My sister went to high school. She is five years younger than me.

And then in Budapest, my cousin told me about Boy Scouts and he took me into the group. I enjoyed the Boy Scout group and from thereon I started skiing, serious skiing. One of the boy scouts gave me an old pair of "briglies" they call them, "boards," you know, and then they taught us skiing. The only turn we made was telemark, that was the only turn, and later on, mid 30's they came with the Stem Christie and then Wedelling like and on to the turns today. We used two poles like today.

BOY SCOUTS, 1937 MARTIN IN REAR

When you lived in Budapest were your skis still homemade?

No. When we lived in Budapest I got some normal wooden skis from one of the old boys. In Budapest there was a company that made skis for the army at that time.

In the Boy Scouts I was every weekend kayaking and canoeing on the Danube and camping outside. Yes. We had about 6 people and the leader in each little group and a total of about 30 in my category. Then we had the older boys.

I was a group leader. We had to make tests. Cooking, get a patch; sewing, get a patch; hiking, skiing, canoeing, for patches. That was my Boy Scout life.

A BATH IN THE DANUBE

Do you still have any friends that you stay in touch with that were in your scout troop?

Yes. Yes. Well, the last few years since I retired here from Heavenly, I went home and we always came together every Monday they have a meeting. Of course after years and years we got always less and less. I have now two, I know they are still alive, I talk to him once but he is going down too now. The other one called me and he has the sugar sickness, very serious but his wife keeps him alive, because she grinds out his food. So, that's the Boy Scouts.

Have many of your friends who live in Hungary come over here to visit?

Once, a couple of winters. They was skiers. Jordache, he came twice. Too sad he just passed away a couple of years ago, and of the skiers too, you know, we have only two skiers who still alive but the other one doesn't ski, only me. And that's it.

HIKING HOME FROM SKIING, 1938
MARTIN ON LEFT

DINNER TIME FOR THE BOY SCOUTS, 1935

The Making of a Glove Maker

I like to tell a story just about how I became a glove maker. Ok? In Budakeszi I went to six elementary school. Then we moved into Budapest. High school I couldn't go because we couldn't afford to because have to pay for books and the things so I went into trade school. And I learned making gloves. I was fifteen years old.

So, once upon a time was a Boy Scout group number 4 Buda Youth Organization. And once upon a time was a Boy Scout leader named Horvathnandi, and once upon a time was an Engeltaler, old Boy Scout, he was a glove maker, and a young fifteen year old Boy Scout named HollMartzie. When we say first and last name, we say last name first.

Every week, Wednesdays, we had a Boy Scout meeting and at one of the meetings, Engeltaler, the glove maker came into the meeting and they introduced me to him and the glove maker asked me, "Do you want to be a glove maker?" and then I was thinking, "glove making, glove making." Then I said, "yes" because that time I didn't have a job, just worked for a grocery shop delivering food and things like this and I didn't want to be a mechanic like my father wanted me to be. Then he told me to get my mother into his shop to make a contract for three and a half years to be apprentice.

After three years he sent me over to the union to make a test how good I make gloves. He didn't make me wait the whole three and a half years. I passed the test and that's how I became a glove maker. And the thing was, when I started working as apprentice I got four bangers (dollars) a week and then after three years when I went for my test, I was getting fourteen dollars. Then, when I passed the test and became a journeyman, I made seventy five dollars a week. That was quite different, yes. Oh, my mother was so happy.

When you were an apprentice, were you working full time as a glove maker or did you go to school also?

Well, twice a week we had to go trade school. We learned bookkeeping and things like this, you know. And fortunately the boss and my colleagues was all skiers so when we had a good snowfall, we meet up at the hill skiing first and then when was noontime we went into the shop. That was very nice, yes.

A YOUNG MARTIN KEEPS UP WITH THE BIG BOYS

So when you were a little boy you skied with your uncle, then you skied with the Boy Scouts, and then you skied with your boss and the other glove makers.

Yes. All of my life I like to ski.

When you were a journeyman did you make hats or coats or anything else or just gloves?

No. Later on I made leather jackets out of pigskin for my colleagues. In the winter we skied and in the summer we sailed. And all the sailors and the skiers they ordered jackets from me. I had the material and a tailor and I made money that way.

The shop I worked for had three shops in Buda and a salesman for out of Budapest. He took orders from ladies shops and like this. We did good.

I worked for two years as a journeyman and then the war came. I was twenty years old.

SAILING

THE HUNGARIAN AIR FORCE, THE LUFTWAFFE & WORLD WAR II

FIGHTER PLANE, 1942

How did it happen that you got into the war? You were a glove maker and what happened?

I volunteered. Well, it was very strange. I wanted to go in the air force. The Boy Scouts had taught me gliding so I was a glider and that wasn't enough to go in the air force. I have to be electrician or some like this. Glove making? Nothing to do with the air force.

Anyway, then I told the guy who was recruiting us I was a boy scout and I know the Morse Code. And that's what got me in the air force. I was a first class Morse. Still flying and fighting in the air. You know, in the air, so I was lucky that way.

So where did you go when you left Budapest or did you stay in Budapest in the air force?

We had different stations, you know, the fighter planes had a different base, and the bombers had a different base and the parachuters had a different base, they all have different bases, you know. About fifty kilometers from Budapest. For two years was in the Hungarian Air Force and then, when Germany came into Hungary in 1942-1943, I had to go, not a choice, to the Luftwaffe because was all German speaking.

A church in a park in Budapest was bombed. The Germans said that the Russians had dropped the bomb but really the Germans had dropped it just to make Hungary go to war against the Russians. Hungary had wanted to stay out of the

MARTIN IS CLEARED FOR TAKEOFF, 1942

war. So after the bombing of the church, we flew over the Carpathian Mountains and bombed railroads and this sort of thing in Russia. And then I was in the Luftwaffe until the war was over. So I was lucky, you know, I survived it.

You said you flew gliders?

Oh, when I was young. When I was in Boy Scouts. In the Air Force I was a radio operator on bombers. A two motor bomber. We went to Russia and bombed Russia. Most of the time we bombed railroad stations to cut down their support. We dropped our bombs and then we low flying over the railroad tracks. Fortunately, we survived there.

How I got hurt once in the air. The Russians was shooting the flak, you know, and all of a sudden through the fuselage one shrapnel went through; went through my parachute, and stopped in my leg here. And, of course, I didn't know nothing. Fortunately we landed and when I walked out of the plane I felt something, you know, blood so that was my only one. I still have the things there. Yes. That was the only time, fortunately.

We flew a couple of dozen bomber missions in 1944 when the big winter came, you know, and was the invasion of the Russians, and they couldn't supply the ground troops. The Russians advanced and they kept coming, coming, so we had to pull back too. And all of a sudden we was already home when they send my whole group over to Germany with the Luftwaffe up near the North Sea.

CLASS A "SKELETON" GLIDER

The last mission we flew was up there. Our last mission was when the Russians came, we had to empty a hospital with German wounded soldiers into a ship and ship them over from Danzig, Germany to Stettin. (Now part of Poland) And we had to go in the air protecting the ship in lighter, two engine, Fokker 58's, yes. It was a plane made for looking for things, making pictures. But we had guns too, you know, three guns; one up, one down, and one in the front.

Did you protect it? Did the ship get there safely?

Well, three planes first they landed because they run out of gas, and the other three planes came to the end station for the boats and were flying over the ocean to protect them. All of a sudden two Russian fighters came and they thought we are two planes but we had three planes and they was shooting and we was shooting and one of our guys, from behind them, he was shooting too. We got one down, and the second one saw he was by himself, turned around and left.

We got the Iron Cross. The whole group, all three crews, got an Iron Cross because we didn't know which one shoot him down. Yes. Well, lot's of fire was going on then in the radio, we talked, you know, and "stay away because one is coming in my direction. You know, don't shoot at him." Oh, that was very funny because somebody's gun got the Russian but nobody know who. So that was our last mission.

Was it frightening? Were you scared?

Well, first thing, yes, you know, when they started shooting then we knowed we had more fire power. A little bit scary, I don't know how we felt. We were just shooting for over half an hour. First they was flying without shooting and one plane followed the other one and when we recognized them we separated because we were flying in one group over the boat, see.

Then when they saw us, they started shooting first and then we started shooting and one of our guys, he was smart, (he told us later on) "two and two is good and now I go behind them." So, ah, that was my last wartime thing.

We had had to go to Germany from Hungary because when the Americans came they bombed everything, the cities and the railroad station and the big factories. They knowed everything, you know, I don't how they knowed it but they just bombed, bombed, bombed, and they came in two dozen planes, Liberators, big groups they came and dropped the bombs.

CLASS B GLIDER

Did you have a sense then that Germany could not win the war?

Well, at first we thought they gonna win but was too late when they developed the jets. The first jet was the Messerschmitt 260, whatever, jet plane. I never forget. Tom, once a dozen Liberators came to bomb and four German jets took off. In twenty minutes, of the dozen Liberators, just things come down and parachuters and whoever could escape, you know. It happened right there above us where we were stationed.

And one Liberator came very low, you know, to land because it got damaged and guys was jumping out and one guy jumped out and his parachute didn't open. It was not far away than from here to Saddle Road up there. We saw him, he banged down and that was it. There was another plane trying to land also, and it landed and one stupid guy started shooting with his handgun, you know, of course… The rest of the guys on that plane just give up and were captured.

Then my commander was smart because he had a map with Russian flags and American flags showing where they was and he says, "Well boys, let's fuel up our six planes and get out of here." So we were going to fly over to a little airforce station not far from Berlin.

Three planes took off first and then our three planes took off later. When we arrived with our three planes, there were only two planes there. One plane was missing. When we landed, we said, "Where is the other plane?" and the guy said that Americans shot him down. After two days, the pilot who had been shot down came into our station. He knew where our station was and the peasants gave him a ride in a horse carriage. That could have been us

AIR FORCE PALS, 1942

MARTIN GRATEFUL FOR A WARM LEATHER FLIGHT SUIT

Prison Camp

Then I became a prisoner. We were waiting at the air station next to Berlin and in less than a week, the Sherman tanks came with the GI's behind them and there we was so we just give up. There was no fight. No point of fighting.

Were you frightened then? Being a prisoner?

No. Well, we just was lucky. You know they came and for us the war was over. That was our feeling. We didn't have to go drop bombs or do something else, see? We was about fifteen people, five planes and the ground group, the mechanics too. They was about 50 people.

Tell me about the day of your capture. How did it happen?

Well, it happened on April 11th, 1945. I was cooking in a gasthouse in the little town. I was making dumplings and all of a sudden the dumplings was ready and I was putting them in the sieve there and all of a sudden a G.I. came in. I never knowed that they coming because I was inside, you know.

And he said, "Germanski, Germanski," (German, German.) And I said, "No Hungary, Hungary" because I want him to know I'm not German and I offered him my dumplings. He thought I was asking if he was hungry and then we both understand. I was laughing. And first he was laughing too and then he became serious and he was asking something, whatever he asked I don't know because I didn't understand, yes. So then he had me go outside with the rest of the guys who already had their hands up. Whenever I make dumplings, I think of that morning.

Did the G.I. eat the dumplings?

No, We ate them up later on. The GI's left and left us alone. After two days, we cut a cow and we had food to cook. We was living good for a whole week. Then, in the morning, a big truck came that held 50 people and they took us to Magdeburg, Oh, there was a big camp, a real camp. All the prisoners from the surrounding area in one place.

Then they put us back on the trucks and we was moving again. We stopped for a little while in Kohlberg. A strange thing happened there that showed me how the Americans was. When I had been at the little air station outside Berlin when I was still free, I had cut up my leather overalls and made two pairs of gloves. I had them in my pack there in Kohlberg.

There in Kohlberg there were French people, civilians, you know but they had guns. They was going around through the big herd of prisoners looking for what they could find. They saw my pack there and opened it and found the gloves. A Frenchman took one pair of my gloves out of my pack. Then I saw him go over to this other French guy and show him the gloves. Then they was looking around for me, I saw them looking around for me and I tried to hide, but of course I couldn't go nowhere, and they caught me and the second guy took my other pair of gloves.

And then came a German officer, a prisoner, with his Iron Cross still around his neck. The French guy, they was all civilians you know, the French people, went over and ripped the cross off the German's neck. The German was so mad he knocked the French civilian down on his belly on the ground. Then the French wanted to stand him on the wall and shoot him but came a G.I. and said, "Whoa!" He wanted to shoot the French. And he put the German officer right away in the first semi truck to haul him out. How lucky he was, yes.

That was a good thing about the Americans, they was, you know, no war anymore why they want to still shooting there in the prison camp? So there was another good story also.

That was the first thing I know about the Americans. They was always fair. Also they always talk so good about America. After the war, that is why I want to live in America. Because of how the GI's were.

Were you ever afraid when you were a prisoner that they were going to kill you?

No. No. We was glad, you know, it's over now. They didn't bother us. They just looked if we had weapons or something. We didn't have any weapons. The guns we never used them. The air force never had any guns but hand guns. And we don't use our hand guns. We left them in the barracks. So we never was worried.

OK, Then in the afternoon bigger trucks came; semi's that held one hundred people. They hauled us into a bigger city where we spent part of a day.

From there we went to Rheinburg camp, still in Germany. It was a huge camp; as big as Carson Valley if you look down from Heavenly. The whole valley full of prisoners. There was a big snow. We were outside laying on the ground there. We had one little K ration box for four people. You couldn't warm them up.

Here is a good story also. There was a colored guy, a G.I. guard, outside our area. And I said, "Mister, Mister, hungry, hungry, cooking, cooking," in German you know, and then, "fire, fire." "Fire" is fire to him too so he looked at me and he knowed what I wanted and he took out his bayonet and cut kindling out of a dead tree was laying there. Then he took out his lighter and lit the kindling for us.

Oh, that was good. The fire was good and we warm up the water first and put in dehydrated cabbages to make it warm to chew. So that was our first warm food.

We lived outside in the snow for about two weeks. The older Germans died of the cold. We saw them carry them out.

Another thing, at first we wasn't fenced in. After two days, big trucks came. The first truck had an auger, the next truck had the poles, and the third truck had the barbed wire. In a half a day we was fenced in.

Anyway, in a few days they took us back to the railroad station and they hauled us through Belgium to Cherbourg, France. Oh, that was something. Travelling through Caen, a big city. Everything was in ruins from the bombing.

In Cherbourg we had big tents. Twenty people in a tent. And when we was marching in, I heard, "Martzie! Martzie!" It was my cousin from Budakeszi. And I yelled, "Yoshka, Yoshka" and he yelled, "No, I'm Tony." Tony and Yoshka were brothers and they looked alike.

Oh, I was so happy to see him, and then they put me as a leader for one tent because I talked German, you know, and then I said, "Can I have this guy with me, my cousin?" and they said no problem so then Tony was in my tent too. The whole group was all Hungarians. They kept us together. We were in Cherbourg for six months. My cousin was lucky. He had been in the S.S. but the GI's never found out.

Did the twenty of you have beds in the tent?

Oh no. We slept on the ground. They give us blankets, army blankets. And then they give us an oven with a chimney going up. Our fire was cardboard. Whatever came cardboard, you know, and wood from boxes.

I was so lucky because they put me in charge of receiving the food down at the shipyard. They emptied the food in big pickup trucks and hauled it up to the camp. Our job was looking what is in it, whatever was in it, making sure it was for the kitchen. Then the cooks came and asked: "What was the menu? What was the menu?" and it was always the same every day. There's no doubt the cabbage, the milk powder, and the egg powder, and the bakers delivered the bread. And then I was there when they was receiving the bread. They came with a sack and said, "OK, how many people are here?" And wherever the Hungarians stayed I always give a couple of extra loaves.

One of the things we had to do in Cherbourg was drive down to the shore to pick up all the old ammunition shells. On Omaha beach we picked up half a truckload of shells and one of our fellows was a coppersmith. He made all kinds of things from those shells. Horses, animals, antlers, things we would give to the GI's. They liked them and treated us well.

One day we was in Cherbourg at the docks picking up the food. The crane lowered the cases down and we loaded them into the trucks. I saw a box labeled "Chocolates." There was a guard there. "Mister, Mister," I said and pointed at the box, "Chocolates, Chocolates." The guard came over and broke the case open so everybody, including the guard got a bunch of chocolate. That was good.

What did you do during the day? Could you go out of the tent?

Oh, we was walking around inside of the camp. Maybe you see some friends. I was looking for my pilot but couldn't find him because the officers they took somewhere else. The GI's was looking for the S.S. people. The newcomers. They had a tattoo.

For a prison camp, Cherbourg was perfect. We had a kitchen. When we got the kitchen, the cook boiled potatoes. Each tent got one bucket of potatoes. And then they brought more food too.

The GI's there made lots of fun for themselves and for us too. They would light a cigarette up in the guard tower and would take one puff and then throw the cigarette down to us. It was very funny. A dozen guys for one cigarette. They was laughing. They had to have some fun too.

At that camp, I was always at the front gate. Every morning they came for working somewhere. There I was with another guy, they needed two guys, volunteers, and there was a big pickup truck and they say: "OK, hop on". We did and they took us into town to a big warehouse and we had to load up the truck with tires. Then we drove somewhere else and the GI's got rid of them on the black market. Money was not worth much at the time so they sold them for money but also whatever they had; soaps, you know.

Then, on the way back to the prison camp, we stopped at a whorehouse. The GI's went in and then one of them said: "Come on" so we went in too. The funniest thing was, the girls there were for the French army from Morocco and they had shaved their bodies. Oh Tom, that was something. Oh, yes. That was the best thing about the GI's. They handled us so nicely, you know.

After the first six months in Cherbourg, they start hauling people home. One troop had left already and then, all of a sudden, they stopped hauling people out because the French railroad people had gone on strike. So we got stuck. They had hauled us all the way to Mailly Le Camp which was close to Paris. And so we were stuck there for another six months.

And there came the winter. Oh, it was the only year I didn't ski. We were in tents and it was cold and raining. There was mud everywhere. It was awful Mailly le Camp was awful. Cherbourg was perfect but Mailly Le Camp was awful. A big camp. Cherbourg had had maybe 500 people, a couple of dozen tents. Mailly Le Camp had long lines of tents, A, B, C, D, lines of tents. I was in D-20. I worked in receiving. It was the worst.

After six months at Mailly Le Camp, they started hauling us home. Our train was loaded up with food and whatever. It took us maybe three days from Mailly Le Camp in France, through Austria and then into Hungary. It was slow because our train always had to pull over to let more important trains go by. We'd wait a few hours or even a day but we had food so it was ok.

I remember when we were in Hungary along the Danube on the train and the GI's was shooting ducks in the water. One of them gave me his gun so I was shooting the ducks too with the GI's gun. That was funny. That GI's name was Bill and he was from Texas. I should have asked him his address for later.

Was your cousin Tony still with you then?

No, he had jumped the train in Austria because since he had been an S.S. he was afraid the communists in Hungary would catch him. He still lives there.

HOME TO BUDAPEST

And then finally we arrived in Budapest. The Russians was there already, see, and they wanted the American food that was left over on the train. Our American captain said, "Ok, what you gonna feed them?" and the Russians showed him soup. But the G.I. said, "no, no" and then divided all the food, everything to us. When went off the train we all got something, a can of coffee or whatever was left over. For us, not for the Russians. He was smart, yes.

There weren't so many people on the train then because the GI's had asked us where we lived and stopped the train to let people off wherever they wanted even before we got to Budapest.

The railroad station was not far walking distance from where I lived, about like from here to the Christiania. So I just walked off the train with my suitcase that a prisoner had made for me out of wood covered with canvas. It was nice. I also had a big sack, an army sack you know, with clothing and whatever. The clothing still had POW on the back.

It was April 11th, 1946, just exactly one year since when I was captured. When I walked into the house, oh, they looked at me. I was wearing a jacket a tailor had made for me out of a grey army blanket. Mother was still in bed because it was early in the morning. Then my sister yelled, "Its Martzie, its Martzie!"

Oh, that was one of the happiest times when I saw my family. Because Tom, close to two years I didn't know nothing about them and they had heard nothing of me. When I had been in Cherbourg I saw a Red Cross paper that showed the bombings in Budapest. Oh, they was pretty close to a place I knew. At that time I was thinking, "Oooo, Jesus Christ, oooo."

During the war, a bomb went through our house. Fortunately the people was down in the cellar, yes. It was the Russians against the Germans in Budapest. The bomb just went through the stairway and made a big hole. My dad was a bricklayer, you know, so he started working on it right away so people could go upstairs.

The next house was really bombed. They had had a bunch of horses in the backyard. Then mother told me they was living off the corpses of the horses that the bombs had killed.

BACK ON THE STREETS OF BUDAPEST

What was life like in Budapest then, the next morning when you woke up at home?

Well, it was kinda calm. There was not much going on. I walked over to the park, a big meadow they called "the Blood Meadow" because they hung people there when was a different war, the Austrian-Hungarian war that was in the 1800's sometime. It had a horse trail all around it where the officers practiced riding. There was a double Chestnut tree there with benches. We picked up the wild Chestnuts off the ground below the tree to take home for the fire for heating. We didn't have much firewood. We had to crack them open with a hammer before we burned them so they wouldn't break open in the fire. It was nice. Good memories of that time.

I remember a lady on the street who sold eating Chestnuts. She roasted them. When was the season, she boiled ears of corn and sold them wrapped in paper to eat right there. The paper bag the roasted Chestnuts came in was so warm to hold in your hands. She made a flat bread boiled in oil also.

WAY AHEAD OF THE PACK

The Communists

Did you go to work right away?

Well, that is another story. I tried to go to look for jobs, you know. Finally, one of my ex colleagues before the war, we was cutting gloves together, he opened a shop and hired me right away. But we didn't work too long, a half a year, because the government raised the tax so high on private business that he couldn't afford it any more. So they had to close it. Then the government took over so you had to work for the government. That was the communists. No private business in the whole country, not only in Budapest. Even the farmers too. They made everything government.

Were there lots of Russians there running all this or were these Hungarian communists?

Well, the Russian leaders came because after the First World War the communists took over Hungary for half a year. Didn't last too long. Hungary threw out the communists and the leaders, they all went to Moscow. Then, after the Second World War was over, these guys, they was all older now and they come back and become leaders of the communist party in Hungary.

Was there a large communist party in Hungary? Did Hungarians run most of the day to day operations?

Oh yes, but it was all for the leaders. They was ruled by the Kremlin. The Kremlin was all over. Hungary, Romania, Czechoslovakia, Bulgaria, the Balkans. But the Balkans was different because Tito was the head guy.

He made his own communist regime. He went against Stalin and they let him do it, you know. All the Balkans, Croatia, was all Tito's. The people was so happy there because it was different. He had his own rules for the people.

The Russian communists they made, how you say it, big wall signs. "People, all for people"… No. All for their leaders. They lived the good life. The wall said, "Work more, you live better." Not the people live better, the leaders live better, so that was the thing now. Food, everything went out to Moscow. The good food, you know, like beef, only the scraps left for the Hungarian people. Same with pork and the grains. They left something just so we don't starve. Who was communist leaders, they had their own stores and shops. The leaders. Down at the lake they had their own big section in summertime, you know, guards around so no private people could go there.

THE HUNK MENDS A SAIL

Tom, I still don't like the color red. Plain red. It reminds me of the communists. Everything was red. Red flags everywhere.

Fortunately I didn't have to join the communist party because I was a good sportsman and the communists they made advertising about good Hungarian sportsmen. Olympians, like when was it, in the 1952 Olympics, lots of Hungarian gold medalists because they were taken care of good by the party.

That was my downfall too. I worked for a government glove shop for quite a while and then they hired me for the army sport club. They had a hotel on the island and I worked for the hotel purchasing. I was shopping all the food, whatever, for the hotel. I had a month off in the wintertime skiing in the training camp in the mountains and in the summertime I was at the lake sailing. That was good.

After three or four years there, I got a little card to come as a witness to a big building that was a prison for people who was against the communists. A politic prison. Not criminals like killers, but whoever was against the communists. At that time, you just have to say, "oh, my neighbor said this or did this against the communists" and then, at midnight, they came and took you.

Alright, so I arrived there and showed them the card about being a witness. "Oh, yes, comrade, empty your pockets, take off your shoe laces, second floor up there in a cell." There I ended up. I was there for a whole week.

The guard came in, you know, and he said, "You wrote on the wall, there" and I say, "I didn't write on the wall, somebody else did it" and bang, he hit me with his rifle stock. I think, "oooo Jesus Christ, what gonna happen?" For a whole week, underneath the bottom of the door they just shoved in a plate. Sometimes was bowl of rice, soup with beans, or whatever just so don't starve, twice a day.

So after a week, they opened the door and said, "Out, come out, comrade, come out!" I was thinking, "I'm not a comrade to you." So in the corridor was a chair so I sat on the chair against the wall and on the other side of the corridor was a window. All of a sudden, a guy came and opened a little bag. I know what was, a bag where they keep shaving tools and things like this.

He opened a razor and began to sharpen it on a leather strop in front of me. I was thinking, "Oh, this is the end of it." The guy enjoyed it how I was so worried about it. Ooooooh. That was what the damn communists did. They played with people who were not party members. Then the guy smiled and said, "Comrade, you gonna go out." So he shaved me nicely and talked nicely how lucky I am and they let me go.

So I arrived in a big chamber. Was a judge there, and the manager of the hotel and the bookkeeper of the whole club. It was a court. All of sudden the judge asked me, "Hollai Comrade, did you receive or pick up two bottle of wine?" "Yes." And I was thinking, "Whoa, what a question." "Yes I picked up two bottle of wine in such and such a town, we had a car at that time, and I delivered it to the hotel and comrade (whatever was his name) he received it and signed the papers and I saved them and once a week I give the papers to the bookkeeper." Then he asked a question for each of them and in half an hour the whole thing was over. They give me back my things and we could go. We all went out.

Now what happened. Next day, I went into the main office at the sport club and I say, "OK, comrade, I just came back to work." And he say, "You was a criminal" and so out... Same happened to the others. Then I started working for a government glove company for another six months and then in 1956 revolution came.

NUMBER 28 ON THE STATE SPONSORED TRACK TEAM

34

The Hungarian Revolution

What happened? One night you went to bed and there was not a revolution and the next day you woke up and there was. What happened? What was that like?

It happened at the radio. The college people, the young people, they went in front of the radio station, the government radio station, and they wanted to read a whole line of freedom. And, of course, the communists they didn't like that, you know, so they started shooting the young people.

And then when we heard that, the whole city went off, the whole city. Wherever they saw a communist member, they killed him, hanged him by the feet in the street. People spitting on him. That was the revolution. Yes. And fortunately, the people got into the communist fort and took the weapons and gave them to the civilians and they knowed who was a communist still running around in uniform and bang, bang, that's how it went.

Then, all of a sudden, two days later, the Russian tanks came, you know, and at that time the whole city was involved. People had weapons around the house and in the streets. They was smart too. We get some oil, 50 gallon oil drums and opened them and spread the whole barrel of oil on the cobblestone streets. When the Russian tanks came they just went around like this, you know, they couldn't drive on those streets and they crashed. Then, when the Russian tank drivers came out, we shot the drivers. The other thing was we got bottles and filled them with gasoline, Molotov cocktails, and then we lit them and threw them. It was so nice to watch the flames flying through the air everywhere and in the tanks they exploded. So that was a very tough time. It went for maybe two weeks.

There was one awful day. It started in Budapest. Big walk in the streets. They captured a Russian tank and were going to the parliament building. Then the Russians started shooting the people down in the street. I heard the machine guns and I ducked right away in the gutter and I saw a little ten year old boy, you know, and he say, "Bachy, Bachy," (Uncle, Uncle.) I told him, "Hang on my leg and just follow me," you know, and he hang on my leg and we was crawling and all of a sudden, I heard the shots. The bullet holes are still there today in the gutter where we was crawling. Then all of a sudden, I didn't feel him holding me so I looked back and the boy was laying there dead.

Martin I hear you tell of all of the awful things you have experienced and yet so often I hear you say, "Oh, Tom, I was so lucky. I was so lucky." You have such a wonderful spirit. All of this awful stuff happens and still you feel you were so lucky.

Today. I still tell it. I was so lucky.

The other thing that amazes me is your memory. You remember when your grandparents and your parents were born and the name of the soldier from Texas who let you shoot his rifle at the ducks. You shot at those ducks sixty four years ago.

Well, I just make myself remember.

How did it end? How did the Russians end the Hungarian revolution?

Finally the Russian jets came and they bombed and there was no more ammunition so things quieted down. Then a new government started, still communist, but they was different than at the beginning. A little lighter. Life got a little easier.

THE CASUAL SAILOR

Refugee

Still, with things calmed down, people started heading west, escaping to the Austrian border. I talked to my friends and my neighbor where I lived and we decided, ok, we go too. My neighbor, a barber, had a little kid, and I had my wife and daughter and so we escaped on the train.

The train was still free and the Austrians say the border was still open but the communists say no. What we had to do was ride the train until the last Hungarian border town. Fortunately, my wife's step-father was a postman there.

We was there for two days and then I was thinking and I talked to my wife and I think, "Jesus, what I left at home in my apartment." I just bought a new three door closet and a nice modern bed, you know, and things I worked for for so long. If I leave them there, they just move in and take over. So I talked to my wife's step father and asked him to take care of Irma and the kids and I went back to Budapest.

Irma's step father knowed the leaders and he gave them watches or money or some worthy thing and that's what they take to see that my wife and daughter could get to Vienna safely while I was back in Budapest.

In a week, I took all of my furnishing over to my sisters and took care of business and then I started going out again the same route but by horse and wagon. In the wagon was an old couple and another guy with a three or four year old girl around his neck. The guy with the little girl had a limp and I realized he couldn't carry the girl so when we finally had to walk, I carried her.

We were making good time. Then, all of a sudden, the pin came out that held the horses to the wagon and boom, very loud, the horses was separated from the wagon. Well, we found the pin but the little nail or whatever that held the pin in was gone. I found some wire in the bottom of the wagon and wound it around and around and that was saved. When I met my step father who lived in the little Hungarian border town, he took care of the guide with the horses and the wagon. Then we walk.

GREAT OUTFIT, GREAT SKIS

37

You have to go at night and be careful because the Russians shot rockets for lighting so they could see the escaping refugees and capture them. In the morning, we was over the border. All of us who had been in the wagon went to a refugee camp.

It happened, at the refugee camp in Austria, I remember they had hot chocolate, I talked to an Austrian taxi driver. I spoke Austrian, of course, so I asked him where he go. "Well," he said, "I come from Vienna with somebody." "Could you take me back to Vienna," I asked him? Well, he had to talk to a young guy who had come to pick up the old couple from the wagon. They had already made arrangements to be picked up and taken to Vienna.

So I opened my rucksack and took out two pair of beautiful deerskin gloves. Oh, he liked those gloves. So he talked to the young guy and he said, "OK, yes" and at noon I was in Vienna. The same day I had come over the border.

You said you spoke Austrian to the taxi driver. What other languages do you speak?

Well, Hungarian and German, of course, and Russian and finally English.

Your wife and daughter were in Vienna?

I didn't know nothing about where they were. Tom, next day, I was looking for work and I called up a glove shop in Vienna and he said "I am not making gloves, just selling them but come in and I will tell you where the factory is."

So I went in and he gave me the address on Chambourgstrasse and he called the boss, Franz Joseph was his name, and told him there was a Hungarian refugee who was a glove maker. The boss said, "Ok, send him in," so next day I went over and met him and he give me a big deerskin, as big as this table. This was a Friday, I had left Hungary on Wednesday, and I was working. I was so lucky.

I started working on the deerskin. I waited until it got moist and soft so it won't jump back and then I started measuring it. One pair of gloves, three where was wider, so I figured out I was going to make eight pair. Just then the boss came in and said it was the end of the day. "Well," I tell him, "I just measured eight pair of gloves out here and maybe in the morning I'll only measure seven pair of gloves."

He liked that. So I cut out eight pair and put them in a wet cloth and went home. Saturday I went back again but only the manager was there. A young fellow. I told him I wanted to come in and finish these things off. He like that. So I finished all eight pair of gloves that day. Then, I was lucky.

That guy give me a ride every weekend for three weeks around the Austrian countryside and the camps looking for my family. See? And then I wrote a letter to my uncle in Germany and then my uncle wrote a letter back to me saying my wife and my family was in Innsbruck. The camps along the border were so full that they hauled some of the refugees to a camp next to Innsbruck.

Oh, good, so I went over to the school where was the refugee management and they gave me a train ticket to Innsbruck to go and pick up my family. In the meantime, my uncle wrote to them too and my wife got a ticket to come to Vienna the next day. So finally my family arrived there in Vienna.

My colleague said his father had just passed away and he had an extra room in his apartment and I could stay there with my family if I would just pay the gas and electric. I worked there for four months. I made good shillings.

The first week I went right away to the American Embassy. I want to go to America. Wherever you wanted to go, you can go to and you need a sponsor. So, OK, I just want to go to America. One guy, A Hungarian, I picked him up in a camp and I brought him to Vienna. I gave him my place to live in the school because I already lived in a private place.

The embassy man said, "Well, just hang on, wait, because something going to happen" because Austria was filled up with refugees. Then, all of a sudden, Mr. Nixon, Eisenhower's vice president, shows up in Vienna to look at what is the situation with the refugees. And from then on, they allowed 30,000 Hungarian refugees to come to the United States. So we was going to America.

NO, IT'S NOT A MOVIE STAR

GOING TO AMERICA

I went to my boss and told him I was going to California and showed him the card the American Embassy had sent me. "Oh, Martin. California. Lemons, oranges, no snow," he said. I was so anxious.

My boss had given me a pair of skis and I had already joined a ski club in Vienna. Right away they had a race and I won first place in the old boys. He was so sorry I was going because he liked me.

We went to the airport in Vienna and flew to the United States. They dropped us off in Elizabeth, New Jersey and bused us over to a big Army Camp that was there, Camp Kilmer. It was left over from the war, you know, but the barracks was empty and there we settled down.

From Vienna I had already wrote a sponsorship paper to my uncle who lived in San Francisco. Right away a paper came back and it was signed by Father Broderick, the church leader who had sponsored my uncle a year before. My uncle sent the paper to Camp Kilmer and all of a sudden they call me, "Martin Hollai, Martin Hollai." I went to the office and they say, "Well, we called the church and they don't know nothing about you."

Then I say, "Church? Church? No, No church. My uncle Andrew Maul." So, I don't know how, they called San Francisco and looked for Andrew Maul and they get hold of him. And then they told him, "There is a family, Martin Hollai and the wife and the child, you sponsor them?" "Ya, ya," he says. What else he can say? So they let me go.

They drove us to New York and put us on a plane at La Guardia. The United Catholic Charity paid for the tickets. The U.S. government gave us each six dollars before we left Camp Kilmer. I know I bought a nail clipper and it didn't work. I didn't know you had to open it. An employee there, he showed me how. I still remember, you know, little things but still in my memory.

California

ELÖRE S.E.
TURAVERSENY
1954. IX. 19.

So we arrived in Oakland in April of 1957. They had told my uncle that Hollai and family, they gonna arrive in Oakland, such and such a flight, such and such a time and when we arrive in Oakland, my uncle was there.

Oh! That was the happiest moment. I had not seen him in almost ten years. He had moved from Hungary to West Germany before the communists took over Hungary. He got married there in 1955. He had come to the United States on a boat a year before. His baby, Lisa, you met her here Tom, came on that boat too.

The Bay Bridge then was only single lane. Oh, when I looked at the big buildings of San Francisco when we drove across the bridge on the bus. No tall towers at that time. Just big white buildings. Still in my mind that is San Francisco. Oh, that was so nice.

San Francisco used to be referred to as "The White City" because of those buildings.

After we had settled down in his house in San Francisco, I went for a long walk from the end of the Noe Street streetcar line up and down the hills to the marina. I wanted to see the boats. That was my happy day seeing all the sailboats.

I lived with my uncle for a couple of weeks. The church got me a job at St. Mary's Hospital as a kitchen helper delivering the big boxes of hot food to first flat east, third flat west, you know. I had a couple of checks from work and the church gave me $60 to go shopping at the end of Fillmore Street at the Safeway. For $15, we filled up the cart with enough food to last us a week. I used the $45 left over to pay for the first month rent in our new apartment.

I went to Oakland twice to talk to glove making companies about a job but they only made work gloves. Then Mrs. Pine, the secretary lady at the church that sponsored me, said, "Martin, I have an address here of a glove company, Napa Glove Company." Well, then I have to take the Greyhound Bus up to Napa to visit the Napa Glove Company. And when I walked in the building I saw a guy there doing the same work as I did. Oh, then I knew that was the place.

I had to see the owner, you know, tell him I'm a glove maker. He said to go and talk to the glove maker and when I did and told him I was looking for a job, the glove maker told me he was the only one they needed there. Then he said, "I will give you an address, Parker Glove Company, Los Angeles, Venice Boulevard."

All right, I took any chance, you know, to get a job where is a glove factory so the next day I had two days off so Greyhound Bus to Los Angeles. It took a whole day because it stopped every little town down the highway. So I arrived and fortunately I had friends there, we came out together from Hungary, and their sponsor was in Los Angeles. I had called my friends before I came down and Auntie Ruthie was waiting for me when my bus came in and took me to the glove factory.

They introduced me, (I couldn't barely talk any English at that time) so they gave me a bundle of skins to start working so I undid my apron, my tools, waited for ten minutes until the skins getting a little moistury, and I started working. I saw my colleague looking and then the foreman came and looked too and he shook his head that I was doing a good job. So they hired me right away and I came home to San Francisco, quit my hospital job, and packed up my belongings in three or four boxes and my rucksack.

You could fit everything you owned in just three or four boxes?

Yes. When I came to America I only had my rucksack but my uncle had given us some clothing for me and my wife and my daughter. So I headed down to Los Angeles.

My friends in Los Angeles had a two car garage but one section was empty and had a bed in it and a half bathroom so I stayed there for a few days. Then we decided it was not too good living like this so we rented a three bedroom house. One bedroom for my friends, one for my wife and me, and one for our daughter and my friend's little boy who was the same age.

I worked at the glove factory and made good money. My friend got a job with the Firestone Tire Company. He worked there until he retired.

SOLITUDE, 1964

The Sierra Nevada

My sponsor had a summer home up in Big Bear. For Thanksgiving we went there. There was snow already. To me this was a big thing. When they set the table there, you know what I'm talking, Jesus!

While I was there I saw a notice that there was a Norwegian Ski Club in Los Angeles so I called the number and I talked to the guy. They had meetings once a week so I went to the meeting of the Peer Gynt Ski Club. The next Thanksgiving they came up skiing to Mammoth so I came along with them.

I had my cross country skis so I walked up to the top of what is now number three chair and I zig-zagged down. Halfway down, I stopped and looked around at the scenery. All of a sudden a gentleman stopped next to me and he said, "Hey sir, I saw you walking up. Come down I give you a ticket and you can ride the chair." "Oh," I said, "I'm really sorry sir but I am so tired now walking once up there." "Well, anyway," he says, "tomorrow." The next day he give me a ticket and I rode the chair. The gentleman was Dave McCoy, the developer and owner of Mammoth Mountain.

Years later when we had the very first World Cup Giant Slalom on Gunbarrel Run, Dave McCoy came up and was setting courses for the race. We met again. "Oh," he says, "didn't I saw you down at Mammoth, you was a cross country?" "Yes sir," I said, and then I carried the poles for him where he set them.

Then came New Years of 1957-1958 and they had the California Cross Country Championship in Heavenly. Well, we had to go to Heavenly. We travelled all night New Year's Eve and ended up in one of the little motels, Andy's Place. The next day we came up and started racing. It was pretty tough. The day after that they asked me to enter the jumping to make points for the club so I did. Then we drove back to Los Angeles.

How did you do in the race?

Oh, I took first place. I still have the trophy over there on the shelf.

We came up to Heavenly again in February. There was a Snowshoe Thompson Race. They called skis "snowshoes" when they first came to America. They called him "Snowshoe Thompson" but he was on long skis, not what we now call snowshoes.

What was the course of that Snowshoe Thompson Race?

We started down on Highway 50 by Camp Sacramento, all the way up to the summit, down by Myers and from Myers to Heavenly. Twenty miles. The course didn't follow the highway. It started in the meadow below Camp Sacramento. It went cross country following the creek and up past Sierra Ski Ranch. I hoped I could hold off Wally Rathgeb who had marked the trail. Then we crossed over the highway by Little Norway Then we went in toward Echo Lake on a nice road and then came down the other side of the mountain to where the gate is where old Highway 50 went down to Christmas Valley. Wherever we had to cross the highway, there was a crew shoveling snow so we could do that.

Then, when we got down to Christmas Valley, we crossed the Truckee River. There was no bridge so we had to take off our skis and jump across the river from rock to rock. Then it was a flat route through Myers and along Pioneer Trail. Pioneer was mostly a dirt road then. We left Pioneer Trail near what is now Al Tahoe Boulevard and headed up through the woods toward Heavenly coming in near where the children's ski school is now.

How did you do in that race?

Oh, I came in second. They give me a nice silver bowl. It's there on the shelf.

While I was at Heavenly, I met Stein Erickson who was the ski school director here. I talk to him in German and tell him, "Mr. Stein, I want to work here." He talked to the owners, Chris Kuraisa and Rudy Gersick (they had two other money partners too, Curly Musso, the president of Harvey's Casino, and George Canon, a farmer from down in the valley) and they said any time I come up I got the job.

WITH HIS PAL, STEIN ERICKSON, 2010

LAKE TAHOE

In August of 1958 I decided I gonna come up. So I wrote to Heavenly to be sure I got the job and then I quit the glove company. They hired me as a guy that does everything and I got board and room and $1.25 an hour. The room was the boiler room, nice and warm. I don't care.

First every morning I vacuum out the swimming pool, put the chemicals in, and take out whatever is swimming on top of it, helping the kitchen, peeling and mashing potatoes. All they served was chicken and mashed potatoes. It was a restaurant and a grocery shop and they had about half a dozen rooms.

So your wife and daughter did not come up with you?

No, I brought them up later when I was settled down.

I met a waiter there, an Estonian guy, who later on became a volunteer ski patroller. At that time he was in the college. The two of us took the only chair, Gunbarrel Chair, to the top and then hiked all the way up to the top of Sky.

I worked there until Labor Day. The owner closed up his restaurant and motel and went to Mexico. I remember a couple came and wanted to rent a room even though we were closed. I rented them a room and collected the thirty dollars we charged for the weekend. I said to the bartender, "Well, Dave, here's thirty dollars." "Put in you pocket," he says. He was a bartender at the casinos also and he said I could get a job as a dishwasher at the casino. I did.

MARTIN POINTS TO THE "PROPER" HUNGARIAN SYMBOL AT SUGAR PINE POINT.
FOURTH ROW , SECOND FROM LEFT.

THE 1960 SQUAW VALLEY WINTER OLYMPICS

I joined the ski club up here and at one of their meetings, Willie Shaeffler, the head of everything for the Squaw Valley Olympics, came to the meeting looking for Nordic skiers. When he met me I told him I was a cross country skier and he hired me right away. He also hired a couple of teachers from our group to work in the office.

Years later, Hugh Killebrew hired Willie to lay out the downhill run for the World Cup at Heavenly. I worked with Willie on that. From the top down, we wanted to make the course straight but the F.I.S. said it wouldn't be long enough. So Willie and I put a bunch of turns in Olympic Downhill to make the length right.

I started working at Squaw Valley in January of 1959, first on the downhill run. A forest ranger from Colorado taught me how to use a chainsaw. I was cutting brush and building a bridge across the creek for the downhill course. Then I was building the jump hill, and other things. Finally, after Chubby Broomhall arrived, we ended up in Tahoma building the cross country trails at Sugar Pine on the Ermine property.

I was working through the summer on the cross country trails. We built a twenty five kilometer loop. Building bridges over the creeks, McKenny Creek, General Creek, four bridges; one going over and one coming back. My worst job was we had to cut twenty some long-pole trees for flagpoles for all the nations. We had to shave off the barks, they was all green, Jesus.

I remember seeing those flagpoles. I was at those Olympics.

Where was the flagpoles at Squaw Valley, they had a big tower kind of thing with plaques of all the nations. If you look at the picture, you see the second plaque from the left in the fourth row down. That was the plaque for Hungary but it was the communist plaque. Last year when we made the things marking the old Olympic cross country course at Sugar Pine, we put the real Hungarian plaque up. No more communist plaque. Now is the same as my father's war medal.

Then they put me in charge of building three biathlon shooting ranges at Sugar Pine Point. They give me how wide and how tall they have to be and things like this so they hired a guy from Tahoma, a local guy with a bulldozer, and we was starting. That was my main job.

The first week I was travelling back and forth from the south shore to Sugar Pine and then they put up a Quonset hut for a storage room so we can sleep there. In the summer it was ok but in the winter it had no heat and was so cold. I had a double plate cooker, electric you know, and I put it under my army cot to heat my fanny. I would leave it on all night long.

Finally, about a couple hundred feet away was a house with a tin roof. The owner was the San Francisco Plumbing Union. My boss called them up and rented the house for a dollar a day. That was good. We had a fireplace and plenty of wood. When my friends came up from San Francisco, about half a dozen of them, they slept there too and they charged them two dollars a day.

My wife and daughter were living in the cabin I had bought out there on James Avenue by Third Street in South Lake Tahoe. I was going to rent the cabin but they wanted fifty dollars a month or something so I bought it with the money I was making at Squaw Valley. I still have the cabin and rent it out.

When we finished all the trails, we started working packing the snow on the trails. We dragged a kind of tiller thing around the trails to break up the ice so the cross country skiers could make their own tracks. We would do that between each event. We had built a stadium and a start and a finish.

They gave me an official entry to the Olympics and I had an official truck, a Dodge with a canvas top. For the hockey game between the U.S. and Russia, I took all my friends in my truck. We sat right in the front.

MARTIN AND CHUBBY BROOMHALL AT 50TH ANNIVERSARY OF THE 1960 OLYMPICS

I was at that game. I was in college and a friend and I slept in the car in the parking lot. At that time, the United States and Russia were big world enemies and yet the sportsmanship was so good that the mostly American crowd cheered when either team made a good play. Then, after the second period, Pat Brown, the governor of California, came out onto the ice and everybody booed him. I thought it was so strange that the crowd was cheering our enemies and booing the governor of California.

We had lots of fun with the Russian cross country team. I told them, "I am not mad at you guys, the sports, I am mad at Stalin and Lennin."

Then I met Hakulinen, the Fin who won the gold in the 1952 Olympics. He spoke German so we talked and I congratulated him, you know, he was a big guy even when I was back in Hungary. Later, before the Olympics was over, he saw me and called me over and gave me a big picture of Hakulinen beating the Swedish guy in the 50 kilometer. I still have the picture here on my wall.

Then, when the games was over, we had to tear everything down and make it like it was. The land was private and they had let us use it but we had to return it to natural. Then it was the Ermine property but is now Sugar Pine State Park. I worked until May. The Ermine family came up in the summer. We hauled out lots of stuff. I used some of the wood to build a shed. The benches in my front yard today came from that lumber.

THE FAMILY THAT SKIS TOGETHER - MARTIN, CEZI, AND PRISCILLA

Priscilla, Cezi & Parking Cars

We finished cleaning up from the Olympics at the Ermine mansion and I said goodbye to my boss, Willie Shaeffler. I thought I might not see him again but I met him later when he came over to Heavenly when we had the World Cup Downhill and we marked the downhill together. Then for five years I was working in the casino, parking cars.

So your wife and daughter lived in South Lake Tahoe during the Olympics?

Yes, but they left. She didn't like it here and wanted to go back to Los Angeles. She took my daughter and she never said something. A couple days before, some friends of hers from Los Angeles came up and parked their trailer in my driveway. That was sad of her. Tom, I worked until two o'clock and came home, no trailer, no wife, no kid. Oh, that bothers me. Not her but my kid. Jesus Christ. I was crying for my daughter. Finally, she start divorcing me and we get divorced.

Part of what goes with the divorcing situation was that my daughter, Kati, could come up for six weeks through the summer to live with me until she became eighteen. I also sent her sixty dollars a month. That worked good because for two years I took care of Harvey's plane, cleaning it up, you know, and the pilot he give me sixty dollars a month. I sent it to Kati.

The divorce brought about yet another name change for you.

Yes. Irma decided to keep the name Hollai. My attorney said that it would protect me better if I changed my name so I changed it to Hollay.

You met Priscilla when you were both working for the casino didn't you?

Yes. How it started, you know, I was parking cars and Priscilla drove in and she stepped out and handed me the key. I looked at her and instead of the key I grab and hold her fingers. And she was so surprised, you know. She liked that. The second time she came in we talked about meeting at coffee break. So I went in to the employee's lunchroom and we talked, talked, talked, and that's how it started.

Had she ever been married before?

Yes, she was married for fifteen years to an engineer in the mines over in Battle Mountain in Nevada. She had to spend the summers there in a cabin. She never forgets the snakes around there. Oooo. That was it. Then, no more.

When you and Priscilla and Boz drove with Barbara and me to Sugar Pine Point a few summers ago, Priscilla told a story about your first date. She said you took her on a hike she will never forget. Tell me that story.

Well, we gonna go hiking at Emerald Bay up to Eagle Falls. Ok. I packed paprika, lunch bread, bacon, red pepper; you know, my kind of lunch. She didn't have any hiking shoes so I gave her a pair of tennis shoes. We hiked quite a ways up there and sat down and had lunch. Oooh. She complained already about her heels hurting. Both heels, you know, the blood. Oooh. That was quite a date.

When did you and Priscilla marry?

In 1963. We went down to Carson. At first, Priscilla's mother didn't think much of her daughter being with a foreigner. But later, when we had Cezi, then everything was ok.

Did Priscilla ever ski?

Twice. I took her up to the top of Ridge and she snowplowed down two times. She liked cross country skiing though. We used to do that a lot. I would carry little Cezi on my neck.

When Cezi was one year old, my mother was out. We were living in the little cabin on James. Big snow. We had a little sled and my mother put a paper box on it and filled it up with blankets and Cezi was sitting in it while my mother pulled her around.

I skied with your daughter Cezi today. She is a wonderful skier. She said you taught her.

Yes. I started skiing with her. Carry her up on the seat. Little skis, little leather boots from Italy. We still have those boots. When she was just a year and a half, I made her a pair of skis from broken ski tips. I just put a strap over them so she could put her little foot in it. I gave her broken poles too. She would walk up and down in the street on them. Later on, Priscilla would come cross country skiing with us along the beach by Camp Richardson. I would carry little Cezi on my shoulder. Yes. Oh. When we had Austrian instructors here, she took free lessons they gave the kids once a week.

A SKIER IS BORN

58

KATI HOLLAI

I have always been so involved in skiing, skiing. When I was parking cars, we formed a Nordic ski club. Ralph Funk was the president, Martin Hollay was the vice-president, and Priscilla Hollay was the treasurer. A real sport club. We went for two seasons. I would mark the cross country trails for the University of Berkeley people and the Reno University people. I marked the trails out by Fallen Leaf Lake. I was pretty well involved in skiing, skiing, skiing.

Yes. I remember you said the bitter cold, awful winter you spent in Mailly Le Camp in France was the only winter you didn't ski. That's a lot of years of skiing if that is the only one you missed.

When was in the Hungarian Air Force, I always had my skis with me. They would let me off to go for the championships. One winter we had a big snow. There was a bombing depot about twenty miles away. The roads and the railroads were all blocked off so they couldn't replace the guards every twenty four hours like usual.

My friend Segei, we called him "Popeye," maybe he is still alive in Australia, and I filled our rucksacks with salami, bread, bacon, cheese, and we was going across straight through the fields. Oh, when the guys saw us they was so happy because they had nothing to eat. There was a big report about what we did. Everybody in the air force knew about it.

There are two parking stories about you and Hugh Killebrew and Harvey Gross. Tell me those stories.

Well, I also worked at the airport. For filling up small planes, I got free flying lessons. Whenever the Cessna 150 was available, the instructor would say, "Come on Martin," and we would go up. One day after we had done seven touch and go's, we landed and the instructor got out of the plane. "OK, Martin," he said. "Make another round." Oh, I was so happy to be flying again.

PRISCILLA, CEZI, AND MARTIN

So, for the first time since the war you were back in airplanes again?

Yes. The airport had just a pump for gas. Nothing else. I took care of Harvey Gross's plane that he used to fly in gamblers. I gassed it up and kept it clean.

One day a small plane came in and at the end of the taxi way I stopped the plane and said, "Sir, you want me to fill her up with gas and check the oil?" "Yes, yes," they say and they got out of the plane. "Can I taxi it over and tie it down?" He looked at me. "Can you do that," he asked? "Yes," I said, so I filled up the plane and checked the oil and took his credit card. I tied down his plane and walked back to the office and he signed the paper and said goodbye and left. The man was Hugh Killebrew, the attorney for Heavenly. Later he bought Heavenly.

The same night I went back to Harvey's parking cars. All of a sudden, a station wagon arrived, two kids in the back. One was Billy and one was Michael, little guys. I recognized the guy and said, "Sir, can I park your car?" He looked at me and then looked over to Eleanor, his wife, and said, "This guy parked my plane, now he wants to park my car." That was a nice evening. Later when I was working for Heavenly, he remembered and was so nice to me.

Once when I won the Snowshoe Thompson Race, before the awards, I had to leave early to go to work parking cars. My supervisor from Squaw Valley, Birger Torrissen, a Norwegian guy, had been watching the race and picked up my trophy and brought it to me at Harvey's.

Lou Hardy, who was in charge of customer service for Harvey's, saw him hand me the trophy and asked, "What is this?" I explained and he told me to wait a minute. He went upstairs and got Harvey Gross, the owner of the hotel who came down and handed me the trophy

BIRGER TORRISSON DELIVERS THE TROPHY
AS HARVEY GROSS WATCHES

again and they took pictures. I still have that picture here. In the back of the picture was the cow skull and the flags with "Food, Fun, & Fortune." That was the logo of Harvey's Wagon Wheel at that time.

Your hair looks considerably darker in that picture; not like the silver fox you are today.

Yes, it was dark brown then. That night Harvey Gross invited me and my wife for dinner in the Sage Room. We all had dinner together. That was nice. Mr. Ledbetter, Harvey's son in law, was there too. It was perfect.

Mr. Ledbetter finally told me I didn't have to park cars any more; that he wanted me to greet the customers. Smile, run over, open the door for the ladies. We made good tips.

BIRGER TORRISSON, MARTIN, THE SNOWSHOE THOMPSON TROPHY & HARVEY GROSS

Didn't you and Priscilla drive across the country?

Yes. In 1964. My mother was here. We drove mother to New York because she didn't like to fly. That way she could take the boat back to Germany from New York. We put mother in the Studebaker station wagon and spent eight days driving across the country. We took the southern route. We visited Williamsburg and saw them still making the shoes and the bread like in the old days.

We went to the World's Fair in New York. That was something. They had a telephone with pictures. I talked to my mother in one corner of the room and I was in the other and we could talk and see each other. In 1964! Oh, what things they had there. What was the future. Highways, freeways, shopping centers. Things that today are real. They also had old and new things together, washing machines, things like this. That was very interesting.

MARTIN HOLLAY
PRO PATROL LEADER

Heavenly Valley

SOUTH LAKE TAHOE

SKI AREA BOX AT SOUTH LAKE TAHOE, CALIFORNIA • TEL. (916) 541-1330

Heavenly

I took my first aid class and signed up for volunteer ski patrol on the weekends. In 1965, the patrol leader asked me to come work for the pro patrol. Well, I was thinking, and I said: "If I get a year around job, I take the job. Winter and summer." Wally Rathgeb, he was the manager at Heavenly, he said, "Good. Year around." So I quit Harvey's and I started working full time at Heavenly in 1965; a pro patroller in the winters and some of everything in the summers.

When I quit at the casino, they had a policy that for every year you worked you got one week paid vacation. I had only three months to go to finish up my fifth year. Mr. Ledbetter told the office to just keep me on the books for the whole five years. They was so good to me.

Once Ledbetter and Hugh Killebrew they rode the chair up and Ledbetter told Killebrew how sorry they were to see me leave Harvey's. Hugh Killebrew later told me, "Well Martin, we'll take care of you same as the casino took care of you." And that's what they did.

The worst job the first summer was greasing up the shivs of Ridge Chair. Oh, that was an awful job. They give us a ride up to the top of Ridge with my partner, Tommy Faye. He later became city manager of the streets. We had a five gallon grease can and a grease gun for him and one for me. We climbed each tower, no safety belts, no nothing. You hang on with your legs and lean out and squirt the grease with the gun. After the first tower, you have grease all over you and your gloves and everything. But, we made it. Of course, later on, they made a working chair with a generator and what you needed.

In the meantime, the Killebrew kids grew up. They spent summertime at Heavenly. I remember Billy Killebrew had to work on the mountain. His dad told him to go work with Martin. Ooo, Billy knew I was a hard worker.

One morning the head guy said, "OK Martin, you and Billy go strengthen the snow fence posts at the top of sky." The posts were loose. So Billy and I drive up to the top of Sky with bags of cement, a wheel barrow, shovels, and a big 50 gallon drum of water, and we shoveled up some decomposed granite on the way up to mix in. When we arrived at the top, Billy asked what we were going to do. I told him, "I gonna mix a wheelbarrow of cement and you gonna mix a wheelbarrow of cement." So we split the work. Billy liked that. Since then I was his pal.

Later, Billy became president of Heavenly when his dad died. So that was Billy Killebrew. His brother Mike worked with me too. Michael's real father was John

Gianotti, the president of Harrah's. After Eleanor and Gianotti were divorced, Eleanor married Hugh Killebrew and he adopted Michael.

Any time Gianotti saw me up on the mountain, he knowed that Mike was working with me and he would say, "Keep him working hard, keep him working hard." Of course, we enjoyed the work. I enjoyed so much my work. They learned from me so they enjoyed the same things. Michael liked the work. He still mentions it. "My best time was when I worked with you, Martin."

At that time we had banner signs between two steel posts. One time when he was president of Heavenly, Billy told me he saw a banner with a wrinkle on it. I asked where it was and he told me so I took the chair up and skied down to the banner with my ladder under my arm and my tools in my pack and adjusted the turnbuckles to take the wrinkle out. I enjoyed the doing, you know.

No snow cats then.

Oh no. We walked or rode the chair lifts or skied.

Summertime, wherever was the road, we drove. When I cut trees with old Col. Sam (Huber) we had to hike there. Especially when we cut Galaxy run. From the very bottom we had to walk up to the Toiyabe Trail. We drove around Kingsbury Grade down to the kinda small parking lot at the big turn. We would park there and walk up to the base of Wells Fargo Chair that was below the base of Stagecoach. It took us about forty five minutes to walk up to where we had left the chainsaws the day before. Out of eight hours we worked maybe only six and the rest of the time we was walking.

When you would fall trees did you start at the bottom of the hill and work up so there would be space for the trees to fall?

No. We would start at the top and work down. We didn't want to carry the saw uphill each day. Only uphill once. We'd hide it in the bushes at night. We fell the trees and cut them into rounds. Prisoners from Carson came up and rolled the rounds into the rocks so when the snow covered the rocky area it covered the rounds too.

The chair we put in there was the Wells Fargo Chair for the downhill run. It went up from the bottom down near Kingsbury, way down below Stagecoach, and went up to the knob above the base of Stagecoach Chair. They finally closed that chair after three seasons because it just didn't get enough snow. In three seasons the longest that chair was open in one season was for 41 days. Oooo, it was the best run with good snow. With two feet of snow it was wonderful. We made a trail from the top of that chair over to The Ridge Hotel so they could ski home.

Then we had to fight with Tito. He was a coach for Heavenly and he build the Eagles Nest. Coming down Toiyabe Trail you got to the base of Boulder by going around a trail we made. Tito says no we can't use that trail because it is on his property. They had a court case, Tito and Killebrew, both attorneys, you know. Killebrew had an attorney named Tom Hall and Tito had an attorney called George whatever.

Pepe Greimeister, the mountain manager didn't want to go to the courthouse because he was a friend of Tito so he sent me. And I was down there and the Judge asked me things like this, you know. "Oh yes, I cut trees there," I said. "Finally some gentleman came and said: 'you stop here because this is my property.'" "Well," I said, "you got to talk to my boss, Mr. Killebrew. I work for him, not for you." So we made a run on Tito's property and he put snow banks there so we couldn't use it. Then Killebrew sent his cat there to push away the snow banks.

The two attorneys for Killebrew and Tito, when they talked to each other in the courtroom, they bashed each other. Then at lunchtime in the restaurant in Minden, the two attorneys they was best buddies. First they was bashing each other in the courtroom and then they was laughing together at lunch. To me that was…, you know what I mean, Jesus Christ.

Finally I said, "What you think, Sam, if we make a trail going down to base of Boulder that didn't go on Tito's property?" "What about the forest service," he says? "Oh screw the forest service," I said. "Let's cut the trees now and whenever they down, not much they can do." So we cut the trees and made the trail.

THE MEN WHO MADE NEVADA SKIING
POSSIBLE, MARTIN & COL. SAM HUBER

You designed some of the runs on the Nevada side, didn't you?

Most of them. My last job was through the winter, Comet Run, with Sandy Hogan, she was the forest ranger. We designed it. We hung the trees and skied through the trees to find the best fall line. That was in 1989.

There is a good picture of Col. Sam Huber and me. Sam and I cut every tree down to make the runs and the lift lines on the Nevada side. Every single tree. Boulder, Dipper, Milky Way Bowl, Galaxy Run, Orion, Big Dipper, Stagecoach, Comet, and then finally Olympic Run. Sam was one of my best friends. He had been a colonel in the Air Force and retired when he was forty six. Then he worked for thirty years up on the mountain with me. Thirty years. Fred Corfee always called him "Colonel." Sam had been a veterinarian before he was in the air force.

You introduced me to Sam and his wife at Sky Deck one day. They were both skiing and must have been in their eighties or nineties then.

Yes, they both loved to ski.

What was early grooming like?

In 1965-1966 we groomed the face. I was a rookie. We put some water in a fifty gallon drum and made handles on it so we could roll it. We had one patroller on skis holding the handles and another patroller with a rope behind him. Both of us were on skis. Then we slowly skied down the face so the drums could smooth the snow.

Finally they made big wooden rollers that they could pull behind a machine. Wherever they were going to have a race, like on Waterfall, we had to footpack the snow by side stepping down the hill on our skis. I never forget, once when was lots of moguls on Waterfall Run and we had to make it smooth with pick and shovels. Ooooh. What a job.

When you became head of the pro patrol in 1967, how many pro patrollers were there?

Sixteen. Eight in California and eight in Nevada. Stan Hansen and I were the two patrol leaders. One of us would be on the Nevada side and the other on the California side and every week we changed.

Did you like being head of the pro patrol?

Yes. When they made me head of the pro patrol, I wondered if some of the other patrollers didn't think too much of that idea. After all, hey Martin he barely talks English. That's how I felt. But then came summertime and Sam was my partner and we started cutting the runs in.

Oh, in the winter we had some good powder skiing in the places we had cleared. Orion's run, Big Dipper run. Then, the following year they put in East Peak chair and then we had to cut the downhill run. Galaxy run was a big job too. All the way from the top of Sky clear down to Wells Fargo chair. Seven miles.

When did they open the Nevada side?

1967, when we build Dipper and Boulder chairs. Before that, we skied the canyons all the way down to Foothill Road. Finally we decided on the lines of Boulder and Dipper. We started up on top of Milky Way Bowl. That was as far as the road went. From there we walked to where is now the top of Dipper.

The first plan was to make three T-bars. From top of Boulder Chair you ski down to East Peak Lake. Then you take a T-bar to the top of the knob. Then you ski down to the flat where is the bottom of Little Dipper now, and from there a T-bar up to the top of what is now Comet and then you ski over to Dipper Canyon and from there take the last T-bar to what is now the top of Dipper Chair. That was the plan.

We was staking it out already. I never forget, there was an engineer and we were close to the top of what is Comet Chair now. He had a radio and I had a radio. He wanted to look down and see the line. A tree was in the way. "Don't cut the

HEAVENLY PRO PATROL, 1965-1966

tree," he said, "just cut a wedge in it so I can look through and see the line." So I did and the tree with the wedge is still there. Then, they finally decided they gonna build the chairs.

What are some of the biggest changes you have seen at Heavenly?

Well, what I can tell you thinking back? Snowmaking. It was one of the biggest deals. In 1974 we didn't have snow until January. Nowhere at Tahoe. Not even in Mammoth. Finally, first weekend of January came a big storm and finally they opened. I never forget. Billy Killebrew said if that weekend didn't snow, he closes period.

The next summer we build the snowmaking. We made a little Mickey Mouse dam with redwood 2 X 8's on the creek at the base of Sky Chair to collect the water to schuss down. Then we made a corrugated pipe from the dam all the way out across Maggie's Run and the pressure was so strong that it pushed the water all the way up to the top of the tram. Then we could make snow on Patsy's Run and Maggie's Run. We had pipes for compressed air and for water.

Did you have a lot of injuries and accidents to deal with when you were a patrolman?

Quite a bit. Oh yes. Lots of them. Finally we had the helicopter picking up people. We had just a single helicopter and they build what we called a "carton" to put the patients in. It had a lid over it with just a window to look out. They took off and went to the hospital. We had four heliports around the mountain so we didn't have to bring them all the way down; just ski them over to the heliport.

Were injuries any different than they are now?

More broken legs. Boots were not as high and we had lots of broken ankles too. We had to figure out different paddings and splints for different injuries. One day two boys getting off the chair called to me that a man behind them was in trouble. The man was slumped over in the chair. We gave him CPR then and all the way to the hospital in the helicopter. The hospital took him to emergency room but he was dead. I later found the boys, they was Blue Angels, and asked them exactly what happened. They said just as he was getting on the chair he started gasping. We figured out that the chair took twelve minutes. If he had had his problem part way up, our CPR might have saved him. Another guy died on I-5.

I had to go down Mott's once because we had somebody get lost. Kirby went

further over to the left, Jimmy Lawrence went on the right hand side, and I went down by the creek. Oh, watching to see if the man had gone in the water. We found him dead. He had drowned in the creek. It was so steep we had to drag him out of the canyon with ropes.

We used to use toboggans to carry people but then we switched to the akias, the two piece metal baskets with two handles in the front and two in the back. I ordered them from Austria. At the same time, I also ordered the yellow padding for the towers. When they came, Hugh Killebrew gave me hell. "Why are you spending money for the towers?" He didn't like that I had spent money for the akias either. Then, his wife, Eleanor, got hurt in Killebrew Canyon. I called for an akia. After that, I didn't hear any more from him about the akias.

A couple of years ago I was up on the mountain one summer and found some old metal akias (they're made of plastic now) all rusted behind some trees. I had a truck take them down the hill. One of them is in my back yard now.

You retired from pro patrol in 1977. What did you do then?

Then I was on the trail crew until I retired in 1990. On the trail crew we worked both summer and winter. In the winter we took care of signs, told the groomers about things to watch for or correct, that sort of thing. We would ski the runs in the morning and during the day and then give the groomers a list of things to do that night. I enjoyed it very much.

In the summers we were cutting trees, building new runs and chairs. One summer at Groove chair the sprinkler system hit the shivs that were going to go up on the towers. Billy gave me hell for that. "We can't have water getting on the shivs." "What happens when it rains or snows," I ask him? He just wanted to… well, he was the boss.

Speaking of "I–5" You've seen a lot of different names on the runs. Now we have all these cheesy casino names. Riusutsu was kind of funny though.

I still call one run "Betty's" but they call it High Roller. Malcolm and I cut the trees for Canyon and he told me they was going to name the run for me. (Martin's Run.) It never happened but that's ok.

Heavenly has several runs named after women; Betty's, Ellie's, Maggie's, Patsy's, Liz's. Did you know the women they were named after?

Yes. Ellie's, of course, is named after Eleanor Killebrew Brown, Hugh's wife. Liz's was named after Curly Musso's wife. Betty's was named after Wally Rathgeb's wife. Maggie's was named after Dave Gay's wife. Patsy's was named after Bob Wood's wife. Bob and Dave had built the tram.

There is a story that someone once asked Patsy Woods what she thought about having a little run like Patsy's named after her. Supposedly she said she thought it was the perfect run for her. "It's short, wide, and easy, just like me."

When Patsy died, I mounted her skis in the coffee house. When Vail came, they took them down. Now I have Patsy's skis in my back yard.

Your backyard is enclosed with a fence made of hundreds of skis.

And hundreds of stories to go with them.

THE AKIA

RETIREMENT

So it's been twenty years since you retired. How did you decide to retire?

Well, the thing was, I was already 65. My colleague, Mr. Lee, said, "Martin, why don't you retire?" Five more years passed and I was 70. I went down to the Social Security office and asked what you do to retire. The fellow gave me some papers to fill out so I filled them out and gave them back to him. Then I went back to work.

In a couple of weeks, I got a big envelope with a check for $1,400 dollars or so for the extra years I had worked. I am retired. I gave the papers to Malcolm Tibbetts, the mountain manager. Malcolm and I walked into Billy's office and Malcolm said, "Martin has retired." "Finally," said Billy! That was in September.

Yes. Twenty years. Jesus Christ. Heavenly gave me a big party, 200 people. They had a big tent, food, dancing, and then I had to talk. Jimmy Lawrence says I should make a little talk. "What should I talk," I asked him? "Well, whatever you think," he said. So made a few words. I said, "Well, all my years I worked here I made lots of friends, some have left, new friends came, but I still have a few who are still here." Then I pointed them out.

Then Billy came over, put his arm around me and said that Heavenly didn't have profit sharing during my years there but from now on they were going to have profit sharing for all employees. "You have to work seven years solid through to get your profit sharing. Well, Martin put his time in already." Then he announce that he give me fifty grand. Ohhhhhh. He announce that to the people. And that's what he did.

Did retirement seem to you to be the end of a part of your life or just another event?

Well, in the summers I would still go up on the mountain and hike and see what the trail crews were working on. Sam would go up too. My life didn't change too much. Every winter I still ski.

Fred Corfee was an investment guy in Sacramento and he was married to Ellie's sister, Jeannie. He put the money in an annuity for me. I bought a new car for Priscilla, we had a beat up old Volkswagen. We lived good. The last twenty years we lived off the fifty grand. We travelled Europe several times. We just had a good life. Again I was so lucky.

The whole Killebrew family has treated you very well.

Yes. Very well.

In the 1990's, John Gianotti talked me into the Masters Downhill Racing. They had different age groups. 25-35, 35-45, you know, all the way up. At that time I was racing from the 70-75. The first race was in Alpine Slalom. I did good but I missed the last gate. I was so mad so I decided to forget the slalom and just race Giant Slalom and Downhill. Only one downhill and that was at Mammoth.

I was at the gate at the Mammoth Downhill and the racer next to me is Dave McCoy. Just then his radio called him and the office needed him for something. "Well Martin," he said, "you beat me this time." Because he couldn't race. He is such a nice man.

I was racing for three seasons and in the three seasons I made two second places. That was enough for me. You go sometimes Squaw Valley, sometimes Sugar Bowl, you know and you had to drive there. I always was watching the good guys. They slip the course, watch the gates and look for whatever, I don't know. I never did know what they was watching for. All was my goal just to make the gates. I did OK. Fourth places, third places, two second places. Then I got tired of it with all the travelling.

When did Priscilla start spending the winters down in the wine country?

After we retired. She retired at the same time I did.

At first, in 1990, I had friends coming from all over. The first friend came from Hungary. A good skier. He stayed here with us. Then we called up Bert, another friend from Toronto, a Hungarian, a jumper back home, and he said he would like to come down to visit. So he did. In the meantime, a third friend from New Zealand, he used to went home to Europe to ski, came here to ski with us and he stayed thirty days. Then later another guy from Australia came over and stayed here. So that went on and on and in the meantime Gabor and Andras and Norby, they came up and oh, we had a ball here.

MARTIN, PRISCILLA & CEZI, AUGUST 2009

And the first year, oh, Priscilla enjoyed it, all my friends around here. The second year around here, me yakking in Hungarian, she learned Hungarian enough to know what I am talking about. The third year she said: "You know honey, I'm tired of this."

In the meantime, Bob Woods, he knowed that Priscilla wanted to go away and he offered his ranch down in St. Helena. Bob Woods and Dave Gay, the propane guy here, they built the tram. Finally Killebrew had bought them out.

Bob and Dave were skiers. They spent the winters up here with their kids on the Angels. The ranch was empty so he let Priscilla live in it for the winter. The next year he said his kids wanted to be at the ranch for Thanksgiving and then for Christmas so I told Priscilla that we gonna look for our own place for her.

We talked with a real estate guy in Calistoga. We told him we maybe gonna sell our house in Tahoe and buy a house in Calistoga. "How much you get for your house in Tahoe," he asked? "Maybe $100,000," I say. "Oh, you don't get nothing here for that," he say. Then he showed us some mobile home parks. We found one we liked for $30,000 so we bought it for cash. We only had $27,000 so our daughter, Cezi, loaned us the extra three thousand. Priscilla was happy down there. She volunteered for the Calistoga Museum. She was a docent and was in charge of the money. She had been a cashier in the casino so that was her job anyway.

You know, the last season when Priscilla was working at Heavenly she worked selling tickets where stagecoach is now. The ticket booth was outside next to the parking lot. Oooh. It was so cold. They had a little heater she plugged in but it took a while to warm up. Now it's in the building but not then. That was her last season.

Where is your first wife now?

Irma is in Sun City. She retired after working for a lock company for twenty years.

And your daughter from that marriage?

Kati got married in Connecticut. She married a sailor from there. His company made commercial sprinkler systems and he moved to Phoenix to run their operation there. He was a meditation kind of guy. They got divorced. When her mother retired, she and Kati bought a home in Sun City and they live together there.

Priscilla and my first wife became friends when we went back for Kati's wedding. Kati's husband loaned us a little Volkswagen to drive around while we were there for the wedding so I was driving, Priscilla was in the front seat, and Irma and my little daughter Cezi were in the back seat. When Priscilla and I went down to Sun City to visit, we stayed with them. We talk on the phone.

CEZI, MARTIN AND KATI

What are some of the most impressive changes that you have seen in the world over your lifetime?

Well. The TV. In '53 and '54 in Budapest was one TV in the big communist hotel lobby. On the TV there I saw "the tractor lady" because in Russia the ladies was driving the tractors, you know. I'll never forget that. Everything was advertising communist things. At home in Budapest, we had only radios in our houses. We would listen to the American radio but we had to be careful in case the neighbor who was maybe a party member would report us. That's how careful we had to be at that time.

Was it worse to live under the Communists than under the Nazi's?

Well, Hungary was never ruled by the Nazi's. They just needed to go through Hungary to get to Africa. That was the shortest route for Rommel's group from Austria. To go through Serbia and Romania and Hungary. The Nazi's never had barracks in Hungary for the army. Just an airbase. That's how I wound up flying for the Luftwaffe. Before was the Hungarian Air Force and then the Luftwaffe took over. I had no choice.

When we camp at Emerald Bay in the summer, you have a little metal lunchbox that you said you have had for a very long time.

When I was still a Boy Scout that was my lunchbox. Yah, I still have it. My mother saved it. When I came home from the war, there it was.

Do you have anything else you have had for a long time?

Oh yes. I have a thing from the prison camp. A little wooden box. You have to see this. One of the prisoners, he carved it for me. See the carving? It translates "American Prison Camp." And you see the tents and the watchtower. Look on the sides here, all four sides. Look what it says. Mailly Le Camp, the years, 1945, 1946, France. The top slides off. I just keep old papers in it.

THE CARVED BOX FROM PRISON CAMP

Tell me about the prisoner who made this for you.

A Hungarian boy. One of the six guys who was in charge of distributing the food to the camp with me. He made us all wooden suitcases too. Covered with army canvas. The wood came from the boxes the food came in. We didn't waste nothing. The six of us had a tent of our own. We could speak German and were all air force guys. "Uploading Commandant," they called me. We went to town to pick up food for the camp.

What is your favorite run today?

Olympic Downhill. I enjoy all my turns there. Galaxy in Nevada and Liz's in California.. At the very beginning when we cut Liz's run we had to make zigzag because the forest service wanted to be able to see that it was a run from the other side of the lake. But years went by and we just cut the zags off. Zags off here, zags off there, and finally we made the nice turns you ski now. Nice fall line.

You have travelled quite a bit since you retired.

Yes, went to Europe for four months even before I retired. We went everywhere in our little Volkswagen bug, camping everywhere. We were gone so long that Pepe Greimeister said Hugh Killebrew was asking, "What happened to Martin?"

Another time we went to Mexico in 1967. In Guaymas, we went down to the harbor and had a man take us along the coast in a little boat. When he learned I was from Hungary, he said he wouldn't charge us for the trip because he liked Hungary so much. That was something. I was so surprised.

Last week at the Bring Gourmet or Go Away party in Sky Meadow, you and I talked with a young border whose grandfather had thrown the ski into the tree on Roundabout. The boy didn't know the story. Tell me about that ski.

Well, his grandfather, Chuck, was a patrolman with kind of a hot temper. One afternoon he was making a sweep down Roundabout and he ran into a skier carrying one ski. He offered to get the man a ride down to get him down the mountain sooner. "No, no, I want to walk," said the skier. So Chuck took his ski and threw it into the tree. Stop at the big turn where Advanced Roundabout meets Roundabout and look very high in the trees. It's still there.

Tonight we are going to Big Bob Tara's memorial service. How long was Bob a patroller?

Malcolm (Tibbetts) hired him. He came from the same town as Malcolm. Bob was a great member of the patrol. A powerful man. "Powder Rhino" some of the fellows called him.

THE BOYS. GABOR, NORBY, MARTIN AND LAZLO

MARTIN IS CHOSEN TO DELIVER THE 2006 OLYMPIC TORCH ON SKIIS

You have some huge, lighted, Olympic rings hanging in your back yard. I was part of that caper. The night you skied the Olympic torch across Heavenly on its way to the Salt Lake City Olympics, those rings were suspended from one of the trams high above World Cup run. After the ceremony, the tram came down and the rings were removed and set aside. Urged on by a good deal of booze, some of the Tahoe Regional Party Authority members spirited them off and put them in your front yard.

The next morning, troubled with a little guilt, one of the guys called Malcolm to tell him what had happened and where the rings were. "Who deserves them more than Martin," asked Malcolm? "Let's leave them there."

I remember walking into the Christiania bar that night after the torch ceremony and you were sitting on a bar stool in your white Olympic suit, holding your torch and surrounded by about a dozen women, all "oohing" and "ahhing." You were the only person in the United States to carry the torch on skis.

Oh, that was a night. I remember Denise Moore gave me a big kiss.

Some time later, Tony Gooding, the ski instructor for the kids in the Heavenly Foundation had you come to the awards ceremony for the kids and asked you to wear your Olympic suit and carry the torch. He played the Olympic anthem and everything.

Yes. I went in and congratulated the youngsters and told them when they grow up hopefully they become a torch bearer or making a medal in the Olympics.

After you skied the torch, you and Boz and John Holman drove to the Salt Lake City Olympics. What all did you see there?

They went to watch the jumping and the downhill and I went to see the biathlon. I was with Norby and his wife. We went to the gate and there was a lot of security there so I asked the guy at the gate if I could see Dr. Broomhall. "Chubby," he yelled? "Take these people over to see Chubby." The fellow took us over to see Chubby and we watched the biathlon and had a nice visit.

Later we went to Stein Erickson's lodge at Deer Valley. I asked the lady in the office there if she had received the white leather gloves I had sent for Stein to celebrate the 50th anniversary of his Olympic Gold Medal in Oslo. She said that Stein had received them.

Norby and Paulette and I went out of the office and sat down to have lunch. The lady we had spoken to about the gloves told Stein we was here and he came over to our table and he and his wife sat down and had lunch with us. Stein asked me if I knew Dr. Steadman. I told him that I did and Stein pointed out that Steadman was walking along outside the restaurant. I excused myself and stepped out to say hello. "Hi Doc," I said. "Oh, hello Martin," he said. "What are you doing here?" "Having lunch with Stein," I said, so Dr. Steadman and his wife came in and joined us all for lunch.

After lunch Dr. Steadman asked how I was doing. I told him my knee was bothering me so he asked his wife to give me their phone number so I could call for an appointment. A month later I called and made an appointment. Boz drove me to Vail so that Steadman could treat me.

So after you retired, you would hike in the summers and ski in the winters. How did you get to know the Tahoe Regional Party Authority gang?

It just happened. Sky Deck. A big group there. I was skating out on the back road and Dennis Wright, who had done blasting for lift towers with me years before, called out. "Martin, hey come here." So I took off my skis and walked up and joined the big party and that is how it started.

That's how we all got involved. One at a time we wandered into that gang at Sky Deck. What a wonderful group of friends.

I will never forget. One time when beautiful Debbie Wilson was there I gave her my special Hungarian toast. She always said she never forgot that toast.

No woman ever forgets your special Hungarian toast. (Martin and the unsuspecting girl clink glasses and sip the wine while their arms are intertwined. Then Martin kisses her and injects a little of his sip. The look of surprise on her face is something to behold.)

I remember when Dennis Wright and I were blasting holes for the tower foundations near the bottom of Stagecoach Chair. We packed all the dynamite in, covered it, and then went over behind the truck about 75 yards away to set off the blast. We had put too much dynamite in. Big rocks were flying through the air and hitting the truck. Jesus!

Anyway, then, summer came. Boz said, "Martin, we're going boat camping." I asked him what I should bring. He said to bring my sleeping bag and a bottle of wine. So we roared across the lake on his boat, "Sudden Impulse," and hiked up to the campsite. "Where should I put my sleeping bag," I ask him? He looked around and told me to put it in the biggest tent there, Barbara and Jay Churchill's tent. The next weekend, he told me to sleep in Sam and Debbie Conant's tent. Finally I bring my own tent.

Your little blue tent looks like you have had it for a long time. How old is it?

I bought that tent in 1977 when I bought my Volkswagen bus. When my daughter Cezi grew up, she used it too. She loved to camp. She was always in charge of the fire.

Now when we camp, you are in charge of making the fires. I've always said that we are lucky that there is a tree standing at Emerald Bay as aggressively as you go looking for firewood each morning. You've built a lot of campfires in your life.

Yes, when I was a boy scout in Hungary, we had to be able to build a fire using only one match. We used dry leaves and no paper. All my life I have used only one match to build a fire. I always build a pile of whatever is around with the smallest, driest stuff on the bottom.

You have appeared in two of the musicals we have done here. You have a beautiful voice. Have you done a lot of singing all of your life?

We was singing in the boy scouts. Every meeting we sang a lot of songs. Once, I was in a play. I played a Zulu cannibal. "Human meat, human meat. How good is the human meat?" I have always liked to sing. We sang marching songs in boot camp.

Did you sing in prison?

Yes, we played for the U.S. officers in the Officer's Club when we were in the Cherbourg prison camp. There was a Hungarian prisoner who was a jazz accordion player back in Hungary. An American officer had an accordion so he loaned it to this guy. Another guy made a drum out of a big tin can and I took a canteen and filled it with dried beans and put a handle on it to make a rattle. That time was a nice life in prison camp. The war was over, no more shooting, good food. It wasn't like life in the camps had been while the war was still on. But even in the bad times, we survived, we survived.

One of the nicest things about camping with you at Emerald Bay is the serenading you do around the campfire with your harmonica each night. How long have you played the harmonica?

My mother played the piccolo when I was a little boy in Budakeszi. She taught me to play the piccolo and also the harmonica. I played with a jazz band in Budapest after the war. Then, when I came to America, I didn't play for a long time. Not until I came to Tahoe.

I was thinking about my old life and I remember how much I like to play and sing the old songs. I started to practice again. I would spend a whole evening just trying to remember one song and learn it again. After two years I had about thirty songs.

Were you up on the mountain today?

Yes. Today I was up at Martin's Peak at the mid station and I put up my old cross country skis from the Olympics. One of the tips is broken because I loaned them to one of Cezi's boyfriends years ago and he broke one.

We haven't talked about Martin's Peak. (Just south of the Gondola observation deck.) You mounted the plaque we all had made for you there. The plaque reads: "Martin Hollay, The Man, The Mountain, The Legend" and has a pair of crossed skis on it.

TOM & MARTIN AT MARTIN'S PEAK
NOTE MT. TALLAC CROSS IN THE BACKGROUND

We also surprised you with the plaque Heavenly installed on the mid-station railing post that faces Martin's Peak.

Tom, I tell you last year I went up on Martin's Peak to fix my flag. When I hike back down, I stop at the place on the observation deck to make sure looks good. I look down at the railing and there, between my hands, is my plaque. I cried. When I get home I go over to Boz's and tell him about it and he tell me he and Sam (Conant) and Barbara and you did that and I cry again. That was something.

You were pretty surprised when we gave you the first plaque also.

Boz take me down to Nephele's for what he say gonna be a party for you and Barbara. Then, when we walk in, there is the whole gang wearing tuxedos and pretty dresses and Martin Hats. Singing "Jolly Fellow." What a surprise.

You were kind enough to invite Barbara and me to the 50th Anniversary Celebration of the 1960 Squaw Valley Olympics earlier this year. You had a good time dancing and also visiting with friends you had worked with at the games.

Yes. Bill Brimmer had been the official photographer of the Olympics. Many of his pictures are in David Antonucci's book, "Snowball's Chance" about how the games came to Squaw Valley. Also, there was Wendell Broomhall who had been in charge of all of the Nordic events at the Olympics. We

WITH BARBARA CHURCHILL

called him "Chubby." Chubby won the Snowshoe Thompson Race in 1957. I made a surprise presentation about his winning to Chubby at the 50th Anniversary dinner at Granlibakken.

Did you ever compete with Chubby in any of those races?

No. The year after Chubby won the Snowshoe Thompson, I came in second against the Finnish guy, Tente McCollough, I never forget his name. The next year, 1959, the Finnish guy was second and I was first.

THE BABE MAGNET

How many times did you win the Snowshoe Thompson Race?

I won first place three times and was second a couple of times. I gave one of my Snowshoe Thompson Race trophies to the museum in Genoa. Snowshoe Thompson is buried there.

What is the longest ski you ever skied on?

Two fifteens. The shorter shaped skis are much easier. Look, Tom. We used to ski the face, Hogsback, all the trees. Nobody but the patrol skied in the trees in those days. In the afternoon, we would work our way up the mountain for the fresh powder. Four patrolmen. Two skied the powder in the morning and two in the afternoon. My favorite was always from the top of West Bowl chair down the lift line all the way down to the front of the lodge. But no more powder skiing in the trees for me now. My knees are gone.

Who do you think was the best skier you have ever known?

Malcolm. (Tibbetts; now retired Heavenly mountain manager) Yes. We skied the canyons many times together. We didn't ski Mott's Canyon then because there was no way out of the gully. Malcolm is also such an amazing woodworker. Such beautiful pieces. They sell for thousands of dollars. But he is the best skier I ever know.

When did you first meet Malcolm?

In 1972. He was a ski patroller for the army in Garmisch, Germany. After two years, he moved to Tahoe. He came to see me with his Army coat on. I asked him to ski down Waterfall with a toboggan. He did it without any problem so I hired him.

What changes have you seen, either at Heavenly or anywhere around the lake that you don't like?

I liked everything. I went along with whatever bad and wrong happened. It didn't make me upset. It's just my nature like this.

When did you meet Boz? (Ted Bozovich)

When Dennis Wright called me over to the Sky Deck party.

You and Boz were pretty much each other's best friends and, of course, eventually you lived across the street from each other.

Yes. He always said, "I gonna be like Martin" but very sorry it just not happen. (Boz died of pancreatic cancer in October of 2009.)

You take food to the mountain to feed the Pine Martins. Tell me about that.

I carry whatever leftover scraps I have from home and scatter it from the lifts.

You are one of the healthiest people I know. Tell me a little about your diet. What do you have for breakfast?

Sour dough bread; my own made apricot, plum, or cherry jam I make when the fruit is in the summertime. Peanut butter. Coffee. And after every meal, an apple. Half an apple if it is a big one.

No juice?

Juice is my little stampedli (a shot glass) of plum brandy first thing every morning.

How about lunch?

Always different. One time I have bread and cheese and pickles and maybe a tomato. The next day I have my own made salt pork with garlic and paprika. Other days different things. Lately, I crack half a dozen walnuts and have them with just plain bread. And always for lunch, a beer.

Dinner?

Always different too. Always green. Beans, peas, raw cauliflower, red cabbage, a pork chop twice a week, spinach with eggs, and a glass of wine, of course. I eat small amounts. I know what is enough.

How about exercise?

Every morning all year I start the morning with pushups. I started out with twenty and now I am down to ten. I make my bending down and also my knee bends. Twice a week I go out in my yard and do weightlifting. I used to do fifteen but now twelve is enough. Of course in the winter I am skiing every day and in the summer I am hiking on the mountain. I ride my bike too. Canoeing too at Emerald Bay. This year I want to paddle the canoe with my daughter Cezi from Camp Richardson along the shore to boat camp in Emerald Bay.

You and a friend make your own wine every year. Tell me about that?

Gabor, yes. Gabor lives in San Leandro. Thirty some years ago he bought his house which had been owned by Portuguese people who had planted grapes all along the fence. Gabor planted more. Around the end of September when they get ripe, we pick the grapes and crush and press them. We put them in big five gallon bottles with just a pinch of grape yeast to help the fermenting. At Christmastime he brings me a case of our wine.

You drink wine and beer but not much hard alcohol.

Well, I learned from Boz. A little vodka and cranberry at cocktail time. Then, sometimes at boat camp, I have a little "Mother's Milk" (Kahlua) in my coffee.

You have had some surgery on your legs over the years.

In 1974 I had one knee done after I fell in some crusty snow while we were widening Galaxy Run. I stopped to answer a question about which tree should be marked. One ski broke through the crust and went down deep. The other ski started sliding down the hill. I went home and ate an apple and then drove to the hospital. Dr. Steadman looked my knee over and said if I hadn't had an apple he would do the surgery right then. Instead, he did my surgery the next day. The next day Heavenly closed. All the patrol brought me a card before they went home for the summer.

When they took off the cast, I asked if I could ski. The doctor said, "Of course. Who gonna run the patrol?" The beginning of the season I was back on skis.

Years later, I had a new kneecap put in because the pain was so bad. I need a new knee here too but, look, with my age what the hell you can do? Forget it. When this knee says, "Martin, it's enough of skiing," that's enough.

MARTIN & TOM IN MARTIN'S YARD

Looking Ahead

What are some of the things you want to do over the rest of your life?

Now. Winter time I gonna ski, make my turns as long as I can. Hopefully I can.

You seem to just expect that your life will be happy in spite of what bad things have happened and might happen.

Well, so far was always good. Back home when I was a little boy, we were always playing, you know, so was happy. Then when we moved to Budapest I joined the Boy Scouts and that was all good things. Camping, hiking, sailing, skiing. Good things.

The first amendment to the Boy Scout rules was to "To make a Hungarian's Hungarian and a man's man." Whatever we learned, family, church. When I was making gloves my boss had been a Boy Scout years ago. He would let me off to go to Scout things.

The war, coming to America, my family. I was always so lucky. Always good things.

Tell me about your thoughts on aging? You were born in 1920 which was a very long time ago. We'll all celebrate your 90th birthday this November first. What is it like as you feel yourself getting to be an older man?

I tell you the truth. Now I start feeling I am getting old. This year. Ten years ago I never knowed what old means. That was my feeling inside. My spirit or whatever you call it. But now, this winter, you know, I wake up and it's different. I think about old friends from when I was little in Hungary.

MARTIN & TOM AT THE SKY DECK LUAU
NOTE MARTIN'S TRAIL MAP SHORTS

You told me some time ago that it was nice that you met and became friends with the members of what we laughingly call the "Tahoe Regional Party Authority" because they tend to be younger than many of your old friends.

Well, back home, anytime I went home somebody had passed away or I got a letter that somebody had passed away. Of the group of my old friends, I was the only one who was still racing. One other guy, he was always the champion in cross country and we was the same age. He is still living but the rest of them passed away, passed away, passed away.

Same with the Boy Scouts. I have only two good friends from the Boy Scouts who are still alive, one of them ten years younger than me. They don't ski anymore. Anytime I visited one of these guys, we would have a little wine. His wife finally said, "Martin, no more wine for him." He is the one with the sugar sickness.

You've said that you and Priscilla want your ashes scattered here in your front yard.

Half of mine. Cezi gonna take half of them home to Hungary to be put with my father, my mother, and my sister. Already on the stone are their names and when they born and died and my name and 1920. Some will go on Martin's Peak too.

A year or two ago, you told me that you thought that when you got older you maybe wouldn't ski downhill anymore; that you would switch to cross country only. Are you still thinking about that?

Well, I was thinking about it. I gonna ski when I am 90. It's my life plan. If gonna happen or not, I don't know. I just planning it. Hang up my downhill skis and do just cross country because cross country brought me to Heavenly and cross country gonna take me...

Then you are going to ski heaven instead of Heavenly?

Look, a Hungarian says about the soldiers that when they die they go to the Everwars. Every war there ever was. I think skiers are gonna meet in the Eversnowfields.

Thank you, my dear friend, for all of the hours you have spent telling me the story of your life or at least your life so far. I feel "so lucky" just to know you.